EMMANUEL JOSEPH

Sacred Synchronicity, Fusing Spirituality, Relationships, Career, and Moral Innovation

Copyright © 2025 by Emmanuel Joseph

All rights reserved. No part of this publication may be reproduced, stored or transmitted in any form or by any means, electronic, mechanical, photocopying, recording, scanning, or otherwise without written permission from the publisher. It is illegal to copy this book, post it to a website, or distribute it by any other means without permission.

First edition

This book was professionally typeset on Reedsy.
Find out more at reedsy.com

Contents

1	Chapter 1	1
2	Chapter 1: The Essence of Sacred Synchronicity	3
3	Chapter 2: The Spiritual Foundation	5
4	Chapter 3: The Power of Relationships	7
5	Chapter 4: Aligning Career with Purpose	9
6	Chapter 5: The Role of Moral Innovation	11
7	Chapter 6: The Interplay of Spiritual Growth and...	13
8	Chapter 7: The Art of Balancing Personal and Professional...	15
9	Chapter 8: The Impact of Sacred Synchronicity on Leadership	17
10	Chapter 9: The Role of Community in Sacred Synchronicity	19
11	Chapter 10: The Practice of Gratitude	21
12	Chapter 11: The Journey of Self-Discovery	23
13	Chapter 12: Embracing Sacred Synchronicity	25

1

Chapter 1

Introduction to Sacred Synchronicity: Fusing Spirituality, Relationships, Career, and Moral Innovation

In the intricate dance of life, we often find ourselves navigating through a myriad of experiences that shape who we are. These experiences, whether personal or professional, spiritual or relational, are not isolated events but are deeply intertwined, forming a beautiful tapestry that reflects the essence of our existence. This interwoven nature of our lives is what we call "sacred synchronicity."

Sacred synchronicity is the harmonious alignment of our spiritual beliefs, personal relationships, professional endeavors, and moral innovations. It is the recognition that each aspect of our lives is interconnected and that by nurturing these connections, we can live a more fulfilling and purpose-driven life. In a world that often emphasizes compartmentalization, sacred synchronicity encourages us to see the bigger picture and understand how our actions in one area can influence and enhance others.

At the heart of sacred synchronicity lies the concept of spirituality. Spirituality is not confined to religious practices but encompasses a broader understanding of our connection to something greater than ourselves. It is the quest for meaning, purpose, and a sense of belonging in the vast cosmos. By cultivating our spirituality, we develop a deeper awareness of our inner selves and our place in the world, which in turn influences our relationships and professional choices.

Our relationships, whether with family, friends, or colleagues, are the vessels through which sacred synchronicity flows. These connections are not merely social interactions but spiritual partnerships that contribute to our growth and evolution. By approaching our relationships with mindfulness, compassion, and a sense of shared purpose, we create a supportive environment that fosters mutual growth and understanding.

Our careers are another vital aspect of sacred synchronicity. When we align our professional pursuits with our spiritual values, work becomes more than just a means of earning a living. It transforms into a vocation that fulfills our deepest desires and contributes to the greater good. This alignment not only brings personal satisfaction but also drives us to innovate ethically, creating positive impact in the world.

Moral innovation is the culmination of sacred synchronicity. It is the application of our spiritual insights and ethical values to solve complex problems and create a better world. Moral innovators are guided by a sense of higher purpose and are committed to making a difference. They recognize that true innovation is not just about technological advancement but about fostering a more just, compassionate, and sustainable world.

"Sacred Synchronicity: Fusing Spirituality, Relationships, Career, and Moral Innovation" is an exploration of this interconnectedness. Through twelve chapters, we will delve into the essence of sacred synchronicity, uncovering how we can integrate spirituality into our daily lives, nurture meaningful relationships, pursue fulfilling careers, and drive moral innovation. This journey invites you to embrace the sacred synchronicity that underlies your existence and to live a life that is both meaningful and impactful.

2

Chapter 1: The Essence of Sacred Synchronicity

In the tapestry of existence, there lies a profound interconnectedness that binds every thread of our lives together. This invisible thread, which we often overlook, weaves spirituality, relationships, career, and moral innovation into a coherent whole. Sacred synchronicity is not merely a concept but a lived experience where the spiritual and the material realms harmoniously converge. It is the realization that our spiritual growth influences our relationships, fuels our career choices, and drives our commitment to ethical innovation.

The journey to understanding sacred synchronicity begins with an exploration of the self. It requires a deep dive into our innermost beliefs, values, and aspirations. As we peel away the layers of superficiality, we discover a core that is intrinsically connected to the universe. This core, often referred to as the soul or spirit, is the source of our true purpose and meaning in life. Recognizing this connection is the first step towards living a life of sacred synchronicity.

In relationships, sacred synchronicity manifests as a deep, almost mystical bond with others. It is the recognition that our interactions with others are not random but are imbued with a higher purpose. This realization transforms our relationships from mere social transactions to profound spiritual partnerships. It encourages us to approach each relationship with mindfulness, compassion, and a sense of shared destiny.

Our careers, too, are a reflection of sacred synchronicity. When we align our professional pursuits with our spiritual values, work becomes more than just a means of livelihood. It transforms into a vocation, a calling that fulfills our deepest desires and contributes to the greater good. This alignment not only brings personal satisfaction but also drives us to innovate ethically, creating positive impact in the world.

Moral innovation is the ultimate expression of sacred synchronicity. It is the application of our spiritual insights and ethical values to solve complex problems and create a better world. Moral innovators are guided by a sense of higher purpose and are committed to making a difference. They recognize that true innovation is not just about technological advancement but about fostering a more just, compassionate, and sustainable world.

3

Chapter 2: The Spiritual Foundation

The foundation of sacred synchronicity is a deep and abiding spirituality. This spirituality is not confined to religious practices but encompasses a broader understanding of the divine and the transcendent. It is an inner journey that leads to a profound sense of connectedness with the universe and a recognition of the sacred in all aspects of life.

Spirituality begins with self-awareness. It involves a continuous process of introspection and reflection, where we examine our thoughts, emotions, and actions. Through practices like meditation, prayer, and contemplation, we develop a deeper understanding of ourselves and our place in the world. This self-awareness is the bedrock of spiritual growth and is essential for living a life of sacred synchronicity.

A key aspect of spirituality is the cultivation of virtues such as compassion, gratitude, and humility. These virtues are not only essential for our personal growth but also for our interactions with others. Compassion allows us to connect with others on a deeper level, while gratitude fosters a sense of appreciation for the blessings in our lives. Humility, on the other hand, keeps us grounded and reminds us of our interconnectedness with all of creation.

Spirituality also involves a commitment to continuous growth and learning. It is a journey that never ends, as there is always more to discover and understand. This commitment to growth is what drives us to seek new experiences, expand our knowledge, and deepen our spiritual practices. It is through this continuous journey that we become more attuned to the sacred synchronicity that pervades our lives.

Ultimately, spirituality is about living in alignment with our highest values and aspirations. It is about being true to ourselves and our deepest convictions. This authenticity is what enables us to live a life of purpose and meaning. When we live in alignment with our spiritual values, we experience a sense of harmony and balance that permeates every aspect of our lives, leading to a life of sacred synchronicity.

4

Chapter 3: The Power of Relationships

Relationships are the crucibles in which sacred synchronicity is forged. They are the mirrors that reflect our deepest truths and the arenas where our spiritual values are tested and refined. In the context of sacred synchronicity, relationships are not just connections with others but are spiritual partnerships that contribute to our growth and evolution.

At the heart of sacred relationships is the concept of unconditional love. This love is not limited to romantic relationships but extends to all forms of connection, including family, friends, and even strangers. Unconditional love is a love that is given freely, without expectations or conditions. It is a love that seeks the highest good for the other and is rooted in a deep sense of compassion and empathy.

Effective communication is another key element of sacred relationships. It involves more than just the exchange of words; it requires active listening, empathy, and a willingness to understand the other's perspective. When we communicate from a place of authenticity and vulnerability, we create a space for deeper connection and mutual growth. This kind of communication fosters trust, respect, and a sense of shared purpose.

Conflict is an inevitable part of any relationship, but in the context of sacred synchronicity, it becomes an opportunity for growth and transformation. When we approach conflict with mindfulness and a commitment to understanding, we can navigate it in a way that strengthens the relationship. This involves letting go of ego-driven reactions and embracing a mindset of curiosity and openness. By doing so, we turn challenges into opportunities for deeper connection and mutual growth.

Finally, sacred relationships are characterized by a sense of shared destiny. This means recognizing that our paths are intertwined and that our growth and success are interconnected. It involves supporting each other in our individual journeys while also working together towards common goals. This sense of shared destiny fosters a deep sense of unity and purpose, creating a strong foundation for a life of sacred synchronicity.

5

Chapter 4: Aligning Career with Purpose

A career aligned with sacred synchronicity is one that reflects our deepest values and aspirations. It is not just a means of earning a living but a vocation that fulfills our sense of purpose and contributes to the greater good. When our professional pursuits are in harmony with our spiritual values, work becomes a source of joy, fulfillment, and positive impact.

The first step in aligning our career with purpose is to identify our core values and passions. This involves a process of self-reflection and exploration, where we examine what truly matters to us and what drives our passion. By understanding our values and passions, we can make career choices that are in alignment with our true selves. This alignment not only brings personal satisfaction but also enhances our ability to contribute meaningfully to our work and the world.

Another important aspect of aligning our career with purpose is the concept of service. This means approaching our work with a mindset of contributing to the well-being of others and the greater good. Whether we are in a leadership position or a supporting role, we can find ways to serve and make a positive impact. This mindset of service transforms work from a mundane task to a sacred calling, where we find fulfillment in making a difference.

Ethical innovation is a key component of a career aligned with sacred synchronicity. This involves using our skills and talents to create solutions that address pressing social, environmental, and ethical challenges. Ethical innovators are driven by a sense of higher purpose and are committed to creating positive change. They recognize that true innovation is not just about technological advancement but about fostering a more just, compassionate, and sustainable world.

Finally, a career aligned with sacred synchronicity involves a commitment to continuous growth and learning. This means staying open to new experiences, seeking out opportunities for development, and embracing challenges as opportunities for growth. By continuously striving to improve and expand our skills and knowledge, we not only enhance our professional success but also deepen our sense of purpose and fulfillment. This commitment to growth ensures that our career remains a dynamic and evolving expression of our true selves.

6

Chapter 5: The Role of Moral Innovation

Moral innovation is the application of our spiritual insights and ethical values to create solutions that address complex problems and foster a better world. It is the recognition that true innovation goes beyond technological advancement and includes the ethical implications of our actions. Moral innovators are guided by a sense of higher purpose and are committed to making a positive impact.

At the heart of moral innovation is the principle of ethical responsibility. This means considering the broader impact of our actions and making decisions that are aligned with our values. It involves a commitment to integrity, transparency, and accountability. Ethical responsibility requires us to be mindful of the consequences of our actions and to prioritize the well-being of others and the planet.

Collaboration is another key aspect of moral innovation. This involves working together with others to co-create solutions that address complex challenges. Collaboration fosters a sense of shared responsibility and collective action. It encourages diverse perspectives and creative problem-solving, leading to more effective and sustainable solutions. By working together, we can harness the power of collective intelligence and drive positive change.

Moral innovation also involves a commitment to social justice. This means recognizing and addressing the systemic inequalities and injustices that exist in our society. It involves advocating for the rights and well-being of marginalized and vulnerable populations. Social justice is about creating a more equitable and inclusive world where everyone has the opportunity to thrive. Moral innovators are champions of social justice and work tirelessly to create a more just and compassionate society.

Finally, moral innovation is driven by a sense of hope and optimism. It is the belief that positive change is possible and that we have the power to make a difference. This sense of hope fuels our determination and resilience, enabling us to persevere in the face of challenges. By maintaining a positive outlook, we inspire others and create a ripple effect of positive change. Moral innovation is not just about creating solutions but about fostering a culture of hope and possibility.

7

Chapter 6: The Interplay of Spiritual Growth and Professional Development

The sacred synchronicity between spiritual growth and professional development is a powerful dynamic that can transform our lives. When we integrate our spiritual values into our professional pursuits, we create a holistic approach to personal and career growth that is both fulfilling and impactful. This chapter explores the ways in which spiritual growth and professional development intersect and how we can harness this interplay to achieve a life of purpose and meaning.

One of the key aspects of this interplay is the concept of vocation. A vocation is more than just a job or career; it is a calling that aligns with our deepest values and passions. When we view our work as a vocation, we are motivated by a sense of purpose and a desire to contribute to the greater good. This perspective transforms work from a mundane task to a sacred endeavor, where we find joy and fulfillment in our professional pursuits.

Another important aspect is the integration of spiritual practices into our work routines. Practices such as mindfulness, meditation, and reflection can enhance our focus, creativity, and overall well-being. By incorporating these practices into our daily work life, we create a space for spiritual growth within our professional environment. This not only improves our performance but also fosters a sense of inner peace and balance.

The interplay between spiritual growth and professional development also involves ethical decision-making. In a world where business decisions often prioritize profit over ethics, it is essential to uphold our spiritual values. Ethical decision-making requires us to consider the broader impact of our actions and to prioritize integrity, transparency, and compassion. By making ethical choices, we contribute to a more just and equitable world and build a foundation of trust and respect in our professional relationships.

Moreover, the integration of spirituality into our professional lives encourages us to pursue continuous learning and growth. This means staying open to new experiences, seeking out opportunities for development, and embracing challenges as opportunities for growth. By continuously striving to improve and expand our skills and knowledge, we not only enhance our professional success but also deepen our spiritual understanding. This commitment to growth ensures that our career remains a dynamic and evolving expression of our true selves.

Ultimately, the sacred synchronicity between spiritual growth and professional development leads to a life of purpose and fulfillment. It is the recognition that our professional pursuits are not separate from our spiritual journey but are an integral part of it. By aligning our work with our spiritual values, we create a holistic approach to personal and career growth that is both meaningful and impactful.

8

Chapter 7: The Art of Balancing Personal and Professional Life

Achieving a balance between personal and professional life is a crucial aspect of living a life of sacred synchronicity. This balance is not just about managing time but about creating harmony between our various roles and responsibilities. It involves a holistic approach that integrates our spiritual values into every aspect of our lives.

The first step in achieving this balance is setting clear boundaries. This means defining the limits of our work and personal time and ensuring that we honor these boundaries. It involves prioritizing our well-being and recognizing that we cannot be effective in our professional roles if we neglect our personal needs. Setting boundaries also means being mindful of the demands we place on ourselves and others and striving for a sustainable work-life balance.

Another important aspect is the practice of self-care. Self-care is not a luxury but a necessity for our overall well-being. It involves taking time to rest, recharge, and nurture our physical, emotional, and spiritual health. This can include activities such as exercise, meditation, hobbies, and spending quality time with loved ones. By prioritizing self-care, we ensure that we have the energy and resilience to meet the demands of our professional and personal lives.

The integration of spirituality into our daily routines is also essential for achieving balance. Spiritual practices such as mindfulness, prayer, and reflection can help us stay grounded and centered amidst the chaos of daily life. These practices provide a space for introspection and connection with our inner selves, enabling us to navigate our responsibilities with clarity and purpose. By incorporating spirituality into our daily routines, we create a sense of harmony and balance that permeates every aspect of our lives.

Effective time management is another key element of balancing personal and professional life. This involves prioritizing tasks, setting realistic goals, and avoiding procrastination. Time management also means being flexible and adaptable, recognizing that unexpected challenges and opportunities will arise. By managing our time effectively, we can ensure that we are able to meet our professional obligations while also making time for personal pursuits and relationships.

Finally, achieving balance requires a commitment to continuous growth and learning. This means staying open to new experiences, seeking out opportunities for development, and embracing challenges as opportunities for growth. By continuously striving to improve and expand our skills and knowledge, we not only enhance our professional success but also deepen our personal fulfillment. This commitment to growth ensures that our lives remain dynamic and evolving, reflecting the sacred synchronicity that underlies our existence.

9

Chapter 8: The Impact of Sacred Synchronicity on Leadership

Leadership is a powerful platform for embodying and promoting sacred synchronicity. When leaders integrate spiritual values into their leadership practices, they create an environment that fosters growth, innovation, and ethical behavior. This chapter explores the impact of sacred synchronicity on leadership and how leaders can harness this dynamic to inspire and motivate others.

At the heart of sacred leadership is the concept of servant leadership. Servant leaders prioritize the well-being and growth of their team members and are committed to serving the greater good. They lead with humility, empathy, and a sense of purpose, recognizing that true leadership is not about wielding power but about empowering others. Servant leaders create a culture of trust and respect, where team members feel valued and supported in their personal and professional growth.

Ethical decision-making is another key aspect of sacred leadership. Leaders are often faced with complex decisions that have far-reaching implications. By upholding their spiritual values, leaders can navigate these decisions with integrity and transparency. Ethical leaders prioritize the well-being of their stakeholders and are committed to making decisions that align with their values. This commitment to ethical decision-making fosters a culture of accountability and trust, creating a strong foundation for sustainable success.

The practice of mindfulness is also essential for sacred leadership. Mindful leaders are present and attentive, fully engaged with their team members and the tasks at hand. They are able to navigate the pressures and demands of leadership with clarity and calmness. Mindfulness also enhances leaders' ability to listen and understand, fostering deeper connections and more effective communication. By practicing mindfulness, leaders create a more focused and harmonious work environment.

Another important aspect of sacred leadership is the commitment to continuous growth and learning. Effective leaders recognize that they are on a journey of personal and professional growth and are committed to developing their skills and knowledge. They seek out opportunities for learning and encourage their team members to do the same. This commitment to growth ensures that the organization remains dynamic and innovative, continuously evolving in response to changing circumstances.

Ultimately, the impact of sacred synchronicity on leadership is transformative. Leaders who embody spiritual values inspire and motivate others to reach their full potential. They create a culture of trust, respect, and ethical behavior, fostering a positive and productive work environment. By integrating spiritual values into their leadership practices, leaders can harness the power of sacred synchronicity to drive meaningful and sustainable success.

10

Chapter 9: The Role of Community in Sacred Synchronicity

Community plays a vital role in the experience of sacred synchronicity. It is within the context of community that our spiritual growth, relationships, career, and moral innovation are nurtured and sustained. This chapter explores the importance of community and how it contributes to a life of sacred synchronicity.

At the heart of community is the concept of interconnectedness. Community is not just a collection of individuals but a web of relationships that are intertwined and interdependent. This interconnectedness creates a sense of belonging and support, where individuals feel valued and connected to something larger than themselves. Community provides a space for shared experiences, mutual support, and collective growth.

One of the key aspects of community is the practice of mutual support. In a community, individuals come together to support and uplift each other. This can take many forms, such as offering a listening ear, providing practical assistance, or sharing resources and knowledge. Mutual support creates a sense of solidarity and fosters a culture of compassion and generosity. It ensures that no one is left to navigate their challenges alone and that everyone has the opportunity to thrive.

Another important aspect of community is the opportunity for collective learning and growth. In a community, individuals have the chance to learn from each other's experiences and perspectives. This collective learning enriches our understanding and broadens our horizons. It encourages us to question our assumptions, embrace new ideas, and expand our knowledge. By engaging in collective learning, we contribute to the growth and evolution of the community as a whole.

Community also provides a platform for collective action and moral innovation. When individuals come together with a shared sense of purpose, they can achieve great things. Collective action involves working together to address pressing social, environmental, and ethical challenges. It harnesses the power of collective intelligence and creativity to create innovative solutions. By engaging in collective action, we can drive positive change and make a meaningful impact in the world.

Ultimately, the role of community in sacred synchronicity is to provide a foundation of support, connection, and collective growth. It is within the context of community that we experience the interconnectedness of our lives and the sacred synchronicity that underlies our existence. By nurturing and sustaining our communities, we create a space for spiritual growth, meaningful relationships, fulfilling careers, and moral innovation.

11

Chapter 10: The Practice of Gratitude

Gratitude is a powerful practice that enhances our experience of sacred synchronicity. It is the recognition of the blessings and abundance in our lives and the acknowledgment of the interconnectedness of all things. This chapter explores the practice of gratitude and how it contributes to a life of sacred synchronicity.

The practice of gratitude begins with mindfulness. It involves being present and attentive to the positive aspects of our lives. This means being present and attentive to the positive aspects of our lives. This means taking the time to notice and appreciate the beauty, kindness, and abundance that surrounds us. By practicing mindfulness, we cultivate a heightened awareness of the present moment and become more attuned to the blessings in our lives.

Another important aspect of gratitude is the practice of appreciation. This involves expressing our thanks and recognition for the people, experiences, and things that bring joy and meaning to our lives. Whether it's a heartfelt thank-you note, a verbal expression of gratitude, or a simple act of kindness, showing appreciation strengthens our connections and fosters a sense of gratitude in others.

Gratitude also involves shifting our focus from what is lacking to what is abundant. In a world that often emphasizes scarcity and competition, it can be easy to get caught up in a mindset of lack. By consciously choosing to focus on the abundance in our lives, we cultivate a sense of contentment and fulfillment. This shift in perspective allows us to see the interconnectedness of all things and recognize the sacred synchronicity that pervades our existence.

The practice of gratitude extends to our challenges and difficulties as well. While it may seem counterintuitive, finding gratitude in difficult situations can transform our experience and foster resilience. By recognizing the lessons and growth opportunities that challenges present, we can approach them with a sense of gratitude and openness. This mindset not only helps us navigate difficulties with grace but also deepens our appreciation for the journey.

Ultimately, the practice of gratitude enhances our experience of sacred synchronicity by fostering a sense of interconnectedness and appreciation for the blessings in our lives. It reminds us of the sacredness of everyday moments and the abundance that surrounds us. By cultivating gratitude, we create a foundation of positivity and joy that permeates every aspect of our lives.

12

Chapter 11: The Journey of Self-Discovery

The journey of self-discovery is a central theme in the experience of sacred synchronicity. It is an ongoing process of exploring and understanding our true selves, our values, and our purpose. This chapter delves into the importance of self-discovery and how it contributes to a life of sacred synchronicity.

Self-discovery begins with self-awareness. This involves a continuous process of introspection and reflection, where we examine our thoughts, emotions, and actions. Through practices like meditation, journaling, and contemplation, we develop a deeper understanding of ourselves and our place in the world. Self-awareness is the foundation of self-discovery and is essential for living an authentic and meaningful life.

Another important aspect of self-discovery is the exploration of our passions and talents. This involves identifying the activities and pursuits that bring us joy and fulfillment. By understanding our unique gifts and strengths, we can make choices that are in alignment with our true selves. This alignment not only brings personal satisfaction but also enables us to contribute meaningfully to our work and the world.

The journey of self-discovery also involves confronting our fears and limitations. This means acknowledging and addressing the aspects of ourselves that hold us back from living our fullest potential. By facing our fears and embracing our vulnerabilities, we create opportunities for growth and transformation. This process requires courage and a willingness to step out of our comfort zones, but it ultimately leads to greater self-awareness and empowerment.

Self-discovery is also about embracing our individuality and uniqueness. In a world that often values conformity, it can be challenging to stay true to ourselves. However, the journey of self-discovery involves recognizing and celebrating our unique qualities and perspectives. By embracing our individuality, we create a sense of authenticity and integrity that permeates every aspect of our lives.

Ultimately, the journey of self-discovery is a lifelong process that contributes to a life of sacred synchronicity. It is through self-discovery that we align our lives with our true values and purpose. By continuously exploring and understanding ourselves, we create a foundation of authenticity and fulfillment that enhances our experience of sacred synchronicity.

13

Chapter 12: Embracing Sacred Synchronicity

Embracing sacred synchronicity is about integrating the principles of spirituality, relationships, career, and moral innovation into every aspect of our lives. It involves a holistic approach that recognizes the interconnectedness of all things and fosters a sense of purpose and meaning. This final chapter explores how we can embrace sacred synchronicity and live a life that is both fulfilling and impactful.

The first step in embracing sacred synchronicity is cultivating a mindset of openness and curiosity. This means staying open to new experiences, perspectives, and possibilities. By approaching life with a sense of wonder and curiosity, we create opportunities for growth and discovery. This mindset allows us to see the interconnectedness of all things and recognize the sacred synchronicity that underlies our existence.

Another important aspect is the practice of mindfulness and presence. This involves being fully engaged and attentive in the present moment. By practicing mindfulness, we cultivate a heightened awareness of our thoughts, emotions, and surroundings. This presence allows us to navigate our lives with clarity and intention, fostering a sense of harmony and balance.

Embracing sacred synchronicity also involves living in alignment with our values and purpose. This means making choices that are true to ourselves and our deepest convictions. By aligning our actions with our values, we create a sense of integrity and authenticity that enhances our experience of sacred synchronicity. This alignment also fosters a sense of fulfillment and joy, as we live a life that is in harmony with our true selves.

The practice of gratitude and appreciation is another key element of embracing sacred synchronicity. By cultivating gratitude, we recognize the blessings and abundance in our lives and create a foundation of positivity and joy. This practice enhances our sense of interconnectedness and fosters a deeper appreciation for the sacred synchronicity that pervades our existence.

Ultimately, embracing sacred synchronicity is about living a life that is both meaningful and impactful. It is about recognizing the interconnectedness of our spiritual growth, relationships, career, and moral innovation and integrating these aspects into a coherent whole. By embracing sacred synchronicity, we create a life of purpose, fulfillment, and positive impact, contributing to the greater good and experiencing the sacredness of every moment.

Book Description: Sacred Synchronicity: Fusing Spirituality, Relationships, Career, and Moral Innovation

Discover the profound interconnectedness that weaves through every aspect of our lives in "Sacred Synchronicity: Fusing Spirituality, Relationships, Career, and Moral Innovation." This enlightening book delves into the essence of sacred synchronicity, offering a holistic approach to living a life of purpose, fulfillment, and positive impact.

Embark on a transformative journey that begins with a deep exploration of spirituality, guiding you to uncover the true essence of your inner self and your place in the universe. Learn how to cultivate meaningful relationships that are not just social connections but spiritual partnerships that contribute to mutual growth and understanding.

Align your professional pursuits with your spiritual values, transforming your career into a vocation that fulfills your deepest desires and contributes to the greater good. Discover the power of ethical innovation, where your spiritual insights and moral values drive you to create solutions that address complex challenges and foster a more just, compassionate, and sustainable

CHAPTER 12: EMBRACING SACRED SYNCHRONICITY

world.

Through twelve insightful chapters, "Sacred Synchronicity" explores the dynamic interplay between spirituality, relationships, career, and moral innovation. It offers practical guidance on integrating these aspects into a coherent whole, creating a life that is both meaningful and impactful.

Whether you are seeking personal growth, professional fulfillment, or a deeper connection with the world around you, "Sacred Synchronicity" provides the wisdom and tools to embrace the sacred interconnectedness of your existence. Live a life that resonates with purpose, harmony, and sacred synchronicity, and experience the transformative power of aligning every aspect of your life with your highest values and aspirations.